Reflections On Faith

by

Campbell Miller

Meditations in the Form of Conversations With God

An environmentally friendly book printed and bound in England by
www.printondemand-worldwide.com

Mixed Sources
Product group from well-managed
forests, and other controlled sources
www.fsc.org Cert no. TT-COC-002641
© 1996 Forest Stewardship Council
FSC

PEFC
PEFC/16-33-415

PEFC Certified
This product is
from sustainably
managed forests
and controlled
sources
www.pefc.org

This book is made entirely of chain-of-custody materials

www.fast-print.net/store.php

Reflections on Faith
Copyright © Campbell Miller 2012

ISBN 978-178035-448-4

First published 2012 by
FASTPRINT PUBLISHING
Peterborough, England.

For Isabel

who is my Companion still

Acknowledgements

The poem quoted on Page 44 is by
Sidney Royse Lysaght(1860-1941)

I wish to thank my friends
Keith Evans
and
June Jones
for their helpful and encouraging comments
.
I also want to express my gratitude to
The Congregation of St Columba's United Reformed Church,
Wolverhampton who have been a constant
source of inspiration and support to me.

Contents

Introduction

These meditations have developed as I found myself, almost unconsciously, relating to God, in the light of my faith, the many thoughts which arose in my mind through the various experiences which life brings. Some of them arose from distressing events such as the loss of my wife: others from quietly reflecting on aspects of Christian belief and practice.
If one has faith, then inevitably, one has questions:
if there is faith, then there will also be doubts.
Doubt is not the opposite of faith –
doubt is faith seeking answers.

I remember listening to a minister, many years ago, who told of a young man who kept coming to him, expressing doubts. In the end, his response was, "Young man, if you would shut your mouth, your doubts would die from lack of fresh air!"
The congregation laughed, thinking this was a clever response. On reflection however, it was clearly an ill-advised response.
The only sensible way to deal with our doubts and questions is to express them honestly to God.

But, does He answer?
As I have given expression to my questions in the quietness of my own mind, I have reflected on what kind of answer God might give!
I freely admit that the answers I have included in these meditations, may sometimes reflect what I would like to hear!
But I have tried to be as honest as I can be and the answers do emerge from pondering what I have come to believe after many years of being a Christian.

It is my hope that others reading these meditations may find that their faith is also stimulated and that they, too, will initiate for themselves, more meaningful conversations with God

Beginning a Conversation.

Lord, I came across several children's letters to you
perhaps they were the result of a task set for them in school, -
they set me thinking –
Here are children directing to you, their thoughts and questions;
that must be a healthy and a sensible thing to do.
Here are some of them:
> Dear God, I went to this wedding and they kissed right in
> church: is that OK?"
> "Dear God, In Bible times did they really talk that fancy?"
> "Dear God, if you watch in Church on Sunday,
> I will show you my new shoes!"
> The one which especially impressed me was this:
> "Dear God, I think about you sometimes even when I am not
> praying".

The expression, "Out of the mouths of babes and sucklings" is so
appropriate here!
These children in their innocent, simplistic way
remind me that true praying is not necessarily
words carefully framed and expressed in pious language.
My thoughts often are reflections about my life,
my questions, my relationships, the world of people around me,
the church and such a variety of experiences as they come.
Wherever I am or whatever I am doing, I am so grateful
that these thoughts and questions about life
can so easily become conversations with You.

But it is not a conversation if it is one-sided!
I presume to believe that you also talk to me!
Certainly it does not happen as a voice
that I hear with my ears!

But, I find that in my mind,
my faith is making me try to imagine
what your side of the conversation might be:
I am sure that I don't get that right all of the time,
but I do believe that is one of the most important ways
in which You communicate with us –
through our own quiet reflections.
I am sure that is how we have all these wonderful words
from the Old Testament prophets when they declare
"Thus saith the Lord"
You were speaking to them through their own thoughts:
their quiet reflections and observations
of the world around them.
Lord, am I being too presumptuous to think like this?
I really am not trying to see myself like an Old Testament prophet!

My child, children expressing in their simple way,
what they feel about me,
certainly pleases and gives me hope,
as well as making me smile!
I am glad that these make you more aware
of me and of my unfailing interest in your life.
Yes, I do talk to you through your thoughts,
through your awareness of what is happening around you.
But there are times when your awareness is less keen;
you miss hearing what I want to say to you!
There are times also when,
what you think I am saying, is really what you want to hear!
But keep listening!
Even some of the prophets sometimes got it wrong!
Above all, keep love
uppermost in your mind and your thoughts.

Appreciating Life

Lord, this morning in the TV news programme,
a man who was being interviewed said,
"I am suffering from a terminal illness – it is called Life!"
(actually he suffered from MS.)
That set me thinking!
He is right,
we are all actually suffering from the same terminal illness!
Does that sound rather depressing?
Am I being very morbid and negative by thinking like that?
Or am I just being realistic?
Actually, Lord, perhaps because I am feeling more cheerful this
morning, I want to change one word in that statement.
I feel I want to declare,
"I am **enjoying** a terminal illness – it is called Life!"
Maybe I don't feel quite like that every day:
circumstances, of course, influence how I feel:
I can't be cheerful all the time.
But I do recognise the great privilege of being alive:
of being surrounded by so much beauty,
so much splendour,
so much variety of experience and,
especially, by fellowship and friendship;
what would life be without other people?
Above all, there is also the wonder of being aware of your presence.
Much as I would like to think that this life could go on for ever,
of course, I recognise that is not in the nature of things!
So I want to go on enjoying this terminal illness
which is your gift to me!
It is a mystery – a great mystery!
Sometimes I wish I knew what lies ahead –

what the result will be of decisions I make –
what will I be doing at this time next year?
But, Lord, if I did have such knowledge
would life still be the great adventure
which I certainly find it to be?

**My child, no, you are not being depressing or morbid –
you are being realistic:
I like your substitution of the word, "enjoying".
Remember my words in John's Gospel,
"I am come that you may have life and
have it in all its fullness."
Life may be "terminal"
at least as far as this life is concerned,
but it is certainly to be enjoyed.
Reflect on the words which Paul wrote to his friends at Corinth
After his wonderful words about love:
Loosely translated they mean,
"We don't see very clearly
It is like looking through a mist.
But a day will come when we shall see it all
as clearly as God sees us:
We will know him just as he knows us!
Until then, we have to concentrate on three things –
Trust in God,
Hold fast to hope,
Put no limits on your love -
the best of the three is love."
Be grateful for the adventures and the opportunities
which life has already offered you:
look ahead with eager anticipation
to those which are still to come.
Life is precious –
it becomes even more precious and wonderful
when lived with me.**

Life with Meaning

Lord, recently, I came across an article about "age".
I suppose we all, at times do have thoughts
about the passing of the years,
even though we appreciate that we can
do nothing to alter the fact that, each day which passes
means that we are a day older!
The sad view was expressed, that
"being old underlines the ultimate futility of existence …
it emphasises the pointlessness of life."
How depressing is that!
I find myself wondering what tragic blows
life has dealt to those who subscribe to such a view!
I know there was a time when it seemed
to be the fashion in Christian thought
to focus on the hope of the next life,
more than on this present one.
There were hymns such as
"O paradise, O paradise, 'tis weary waiting here",
as if the true Christian should be longing
for death and transition to a new and better life.
Even in some hymn books in current use
we can find sentiments such as
"my spirit faints to reach the land I love,
the bright inheritance of saints, Jerusalem above."
A lady was staying at a Christian guest house
where her table companion greeted her with the words,
"are you longing to meet your Lord?",
then she proceeded to take her medication, which clearly
was designed to delay as long as possible, her meeting with you!
Lord, I must confess that I find it impossible to share

these kind of sentiments, - life here is precious!
I certainly am not longing to meet you, at least,
not in the way which she implied!
I am grateful for the privilege of being able to meet you
day by day in these conversations which we have!
I am aware that, when some of these hymns were written,
life was very hard indeed for many.
I think also of the Spirituals which have come down to us
from the days of the slave trade:
songs such as "I ain't gonna tarry here",
"Bound for Canaan land",
"gonna shout all over God's Heaven" –
As I remember the harsh conditions in which
many were forced to live, I find it easy to understand
why the idea of Heaven was so attractive.

My child, you are right to remember the conditions
which undoubtedly inspired such sentiments.
For many, life was so miserable -
any idea of something better would be longed for.
But you must also be concerned about those who today
feel that life has become pointless.
Sympathise with their circumstances:
Perhaps they are experiencing a loneliness
which aches for a loved one, now gone:
debilitating illness which has destroyed the life previously lived:
a situation which has destroyed peace of mind
from which there seems to be no escape. -
These are circumstances which cry out
for help from those who have faith:
which cry out for your example - your active support
To show that life is good – even for them!
Remember my words,
"I am come that you may have life and have it in all its fullness".
Appreciate also that, when I used the phrase "eternal life",

I was talking especially about life here and now.
I was meaning that, with me,
this life of yours, here and now, should be wonderful -
full of meaning and purpose.
The whole tenor of my teaching was about life in this world.
Though, of course I also talked about life beyond this one.
Your task, your responsibility as one of my people
is to demonstrate to people around you that
whatever their circumstances,
whatever their age,
whatever their social standing,
whatever their level of intelligence,
whatever they are as individuals, -
each one matters to me: each one is unique and precious.
That is communicated, not by preaching,
not by quoting Bible texts, however appropriate they may be.
It is by you being beside them:
It is communicated by active caring love.
Of course you also must never lose sight of the glorious hope,
inspired by my triumph over death,
that this life is by no means all there is,
but - we talk about this in another conversation.

Campbell Miller

Listening To "The News"

Lord, as usual, I have been viewing the news bulletin on TV -
it has left me feeling rather depressed.
Violence, crime, cruelty,
unpleasant gossip about so-called celebrities,
alleged tax avoidance,
alleged misdeeds of clergy
rising unemployment, drought in some places -
elsewhere, flooding:
distressing stories of hunger and deprivation –
such a long list of troubles within our society and around the world.
Now and again - some brief mention of good news –
perhaps some heroic action
generous response to appeals where help is desperately needed, -
but the bad news always seems dominant:
we feel so helpless to bring about change.

My child, I understand what you are saying -
bad news also distresses me.
There is nothing new about this,
but that does not make it any easier to bear.
Think of the words in the Prophet Habakkuk.
He was expressing his dismay
as he looked out on his world –
he asked me how much longer
violence around him would continue:
Why did he see such terrible injustice?
Why such lawlessness, crime, and cruelty?
Why cannot laws be enforced?
Why do criminals seem to crowd out honest people?
Remember, he was commenting on life

nearly three thousand years ago -
it could have been said today!
Concerns were being expressed about society,
then, just as they are now!
And I was being blamed for it
just as many blame me today!
You shouldn't be surprised that, sadly,
there have always been problems
when people are living together:
nor should you be surprised that
there have always been individuals or groups
who want it to be different.
Be glad when you find that there are some
who have a vision of a better and more caring society.
Be challenged, actively to share their concern.
Too often, Christians are seen to be harshly judgemental –
Sometimes also hypocritical!
Judging what others do
while not being entirely innocent themselves.
If your vision of a better Society
does not include a strong emphasis
on the need for caring love and concern,
at the level of all your relationships,
whether close, or casual,
it must be doomed to failure.

Being in Church

Today, Lord, I have been to Church.
I enjoyed the hymns,
though I must say, there were two of them that I did not know!
I tried to relate to the prayers, -
I must confess, I found my thoughts wandering.
As for the sermon,
I am sorry to say that the preacher
lost my attention almost from the opening sentence.
I am ashamed to say, I switched off!
My mind was elsewhere, reviewing the past week,
looking ahead to what had to done in the next week:
I must be honest with you –
I even had a feeling of
impatience and irritation with the preacher:
"why could he not say something interesting?
Is this that he is saying,
really relevant to the folks who are gathered here?"
Lord, this is supposed to be you talking to us!
The final hymn is announced: I breathe a sigh of relief!
Lord, I really am ashamed of myself for feeling like this.
Forgive me for being so critical:
forgive me for my wandering thoughts.
I do truly want to offer you a more worthy offering of worship.
Sometimes I feel that I have had a wasted hour:
then as I talk with my friends and fellow worshippers,
I feel the warmth of fellowship surrounding me:
these are folk who care!
Some of them actually say
"that was a helpful service this morning!"
my feeling of shame increases!

Apparently the preacher's words spoke to them.
Perhaps on other occasions, when the service met my needs,
some of them felt that there had been little in it for them!

My child, I understand your complaint:
some sermons bore me as well –
some of yours among them!
Remember – the preacher is human!
Why did you come?
What was uppermost in your mind as you came?
Focus your mind on why you are in Church –
not to criticise, but to discover a greater sense of my presence.
You are here to worship,
here for fellowship with me -
fellowship with your fellow worshippers.
Even if you take with you, little of what the preacher said,
take into the week before you the warmth of fellowship:
the increased awareness of my presence with you.
You have not wasted an hour,
but – next time,
come prepared – think of me as you come:
give me a little more of your attention -
maybe, however dull the preacher,
you may well find that there is something of my voice
speaking to you as well!

The Trinity

Lord, I am very conscious that in these conversations with you,
sometimes I appear to be addressing
my comments and questions to Jesus,
and sometimes to you.
That raises for me
the mysterious question of the Trinity!
Do I need to worry about this?
Is the doctrine of the Trinity, just that –
a doctrine – a way which theologians
over the years have devised in their attempt
to explain the unexplainable –
the mystery of your eternal being?
I know that for centuries scholars
have argued about this, often with bitter disagreement.
My faith is content to accept the mystery - indeed
I feel that if I, especially in the context of these meditations,
become too involved in "doctrine" and theological debate
I would perhaps find that my relationship with you becomes
somewhat confused!
But, I do value, immensely, the words of blessing
with which we usually end our worship,
     "The grace of the Lord Jesus Christ, and
     the love of God, and
     the fellowship of the Holy Spirit,
     be with you all. Amen"
These words, coming from Paul writing to the Church at Corinth,
are sufficient recognition, for me,
of the wonder of your Divine nature.

Campbell Miller

My child, reflect on this.
Theologians are trying to probe the mystery –
and they are right to do so,
but it is not helpful for everyone's faith!
Perhaps it is helpful to realise that the idea of the Trinity
did not arise because intellectual geniuses
manipulated abstract ideas.
It came straight out of the experience of ordinary,
down to earth men and women
who were striving to live as Christians:
people who were devoting their energies to live as my people.
It began simply and untheologically as they began to realise
that they could not say all they understood
by the mysterious word "God"
until they had said, "Father, Son and Spirit."
They realised that I had revealed myself
in a variety of ways,
each of them as significant and meaningful as the other.
As they struggled to elucidate adequately, my nature;
as they tried to communicate their experience of me to others,
they found that only by thinking of me
as Father, Son and Spirit and yet, still as One God,
could they adequately penetrate in some way,
the mystery of my divine being.
Mystery will always be at the heart of your faith.
Instead of worrying about doctrine,
focus instead on experience,
just as these early Christians did.
Continue to appreciate the familiar words
of that blessing, which you hear so often:
continue to talk to me, just as you have been doing –
and keep on listening to me.

A Variable Faith.

Lord, it is Sunday – nearly time to go to worship:
for some reason, today, I feel my faith is at rather a low ebb!
I am feeling again like that man, of whom we are told in the Gospel,
who brought his epileptic son to you for healing.
He said he had faith, but not enough:
that is how I feel when I am victim to these swings of mood.
Sometimes, like today I feel you are remote:
what is the point in going to worship when I am feeling like this?
At other times, I feel I am eager to worship
and my faith in you is strong.
What is wrong with me, Lord?
Should I not feel the same strong trust in you,
regardless of the circumstances in which I find myself?
It seems to me that my feelings sometimes take over;
they influence the strength of my faith in you
I am tempted to excuse my failing faith
by thinking that the man in the Gospel had the advantage over me:
he had your physical presence beside him!
It is much more difficult for me!

My child, I do understand.
Clearly, the man in the Gospel
came with some measure of hope,
he must have had sufficient faith in all he had heard about me,
but his feelings, like yours often are, were all rather mixed up.
You too have turned to me so you also are showing faith:
maybe today it is not so strong as it is on other occasions,
but it is still there.
What you must remember is that you are human.
You are also being honest with me and that is so important:

it means you are being honest with yourself:
you are acknowledging your need of me.
Your emotions are important – all part of being human:
be glad for the times when you are excited about your faith.
But, true faith must never be a matter of the emotions alone.
Cast your mind back to the times when you felt
beyond all doubt that I was near,
my presence was making all the difference to your life.
Be thankful also that when you don't feel like that,
such faith as you can muster reminds you
that I am still there and still supporting you!
Be especially grateful that you can always
tell me exactly how you are feeling.
Remember. you are certainly in good and honourable company.
Think of the Psalmist - often, in one way or another,
you find in these deeply spiritual, honest expressions of faith,
accompanying expressions of serious
feelings of doubt and despair.
Psalm 55 is but one example:
> "Give ear to my prayer, O God; attend to me and answer me;
> I am overcome by my trouble.
> My heart is in anguish within me and I say,
> 'O that I had wings like a dove!
> I would fly away and be at rest!'"
These are the words of a man who is certainly
in a fearful and despairing mood; down in the dumps!
fed up with what life seems to have dealt to him;
he wants to escape from it all;
yet who can deny that he is also a man of faith?
For he also declares,
> "I call upon God: and the Lord will save me;
> God, I will trust in you!"
Ponder such words: take them to heart:
You may feel your are in something of a spiritual desert,
But, don't fling away allowing, your own emotions to dominate,

let your flagging faith reach out;
be assured that I am here for you.

Campbell Miller

Disagreements about Faith

Lord, I have been looking at my denomination's journal:
I tend to look first of all at 'Letters to the Editor'
I suppose they serve a usual purpose,
as they have a place in most newspapers and journals:
I often find myself becoming rather angry,
at the tone of many of them.
Usually, while defending a particular point of view
they are condemning any contradictory view.
I suppose it provides a useful platform for debate.
However, I become depressed when the letters
are those published in a religious journal.
So often they are about matters of belief,
written, sometimes uncharitably - in defence, or condemnation,
of a particular way of expressing faith.
I find it disturbing that so often
views about faith are defended or condemned
in such a dogmatic and harsh way:
the implication is, "I am right because I hold this belief -
since you don't hold it,
or you express it differently to me, you are wrong."
I suppose we should be grateful that we have moved on
from the days when disagreements about belief
resulted in horrific punishment and death,
but all this seems so far removed from the idea
of faith as a relationship with you
whose greatest attribute is love.
Lord, "Why does faith bring out the worst in so many?"
Surely with your emphasis on love,
there should be no place for us fighting about faith?

**Yes, my child, it is sad that sometimes
disagreement about faith results in strife:
it should not happen –
what must be appreciated is
that there is always room
for different ways of expressing belief.
Honesty about one's beliefs is of such great importance.
I do not want followers who say they hold a particular belief
because they think it is expected of them –
expected, either by me or by other people!
When the Bible talks about "believing" in me,
it does not mean, "giving assent of the mind"
to a set of beliefs or theories:
believing is not an intellectual exercise.
It is essentially about trust.
You are not a Christian because you subscribe
to certain beliefs about me.
If you had asked Peter
or any of my other disciples about their beliefs,
they would have had some difficulty in answering;
they were often quite bewildered by many of the things I taught:
they would have said, "we believe in Him – we trust Him"**

Lord, I remember reading the words
of one of the characters in a novel
"Our faith is not a series of propositions, which we impose
on people as a kind of entry fee into the kingdom."
It seems to me that we often imply that it is!
If I find it difficult to believe,
for example, in your Virgin Birth:
if I cannot accept the verbal inspiration of the whole of the Bible,
am I still a Christian?
For some, acceptance of these and many other propositions
appear to be necessary,
otherwise, in their view, one is excluded from your Kingdom.

My child, think of the incident
related in the Acts of the Apostles,
where Paul and his companion
were locked up for their faith:
their jailer was so impressed with them
that he said, "what must I do to be saved?"
He was not given a series of beliefs which had to be accepted:
he was told, "Believe on the Lord Jesus Christ and
you will be saved."
"Believe" means "trust":
it means turn your life around by beginning to follow me.
Believing is much more a matter of the "heart"
than it is of the intellect –
it is believing in me,
not believing propositions about me!
Above all, it is about responding to my love.

Campbell Miller

The Gulf Between "Us and Them".

Lord, when I am in Church at worship,
I am very conscious of the many people who pass by outside:
most of them never even give a glance in our direction.
I worry that there are so few of us:
I wonder what impression that gives.
But - most of the passers-by, don't even seem to notice!
It emphasises for me how great the gulf is between us and them!
How do we bridge that gulf?
Do we need to sing more lively, modern hymns?
Do we need to change completely
the way in which we offer worship:
perhaps stop calling it that?
Do we need bigger and better posters
telling people what we stand for?
We are mainly an elderly congregation –
do we give the impression that Church is only for old folk?
Lord, you can tell that I'm struggling –
feeling that we are failures –
failing you and failing the people around us!
We know that our faith could give more meaning to their lives:
how do we help them to realise that?

My child, I do understand how you feel.
Of course you would like to see
a much larger congregation when you meet for worship.
It would bring joy to me also.
But you should appreciate that
the success of a church cannot be judged alone
on the size of its congregation.
Yes, there is a great gulf.

It is created, not so much by those who are against you,
but by those who are apathetic –
who have no strong feelings about me or –
about your faith, one way or the other!
There is no magic solution!
No quick fix formula which you need to follow!
In the world of nature, if there is to be a harvest,
seed needs to be sown.
Likewise, if you are to see growth:
if the gulf, of which you speak, is to be bridged,
seed needs to be sown –
the seed which you need to scatter and plant is love.
Love for others – a love which shows itself in active caring.
There is no alternative:
There is no other way but love –
Not just words of love –
love in action – a church which cares.

Reading the Bible (1)

Lord, I know that reading the Bible
is supposed to be an important part of my life as a Christian.
I must confess that there are many other modern books –
especially novels – which grip my attention far more.
Don't misunderstand me!
I do spend some time reading from the Bible, but,
certainly, I can easily succumb
to the attraction of a more interesting story which holds my attention.
O, I know there are some great stories in the Bible:
I can enjoy them, but
there is also a lot in the Bible which troubles me.
I have been reading through the Psalms:
many of them are really inspirational:
they give me valuable food for thought -
many more of them have the opposite effect on me!
There is so much talk about "enemies" -
prayers for them to be destroyed!
In Psalm 7, for example, you are described as
a righteous judge who always condemns the wicked:
it even declares that if they do not change their ways,
you will "sharpen your sword" and
"take up your deadly weapons"
It is hardly inspiring devotional reading!
I understand your condemnation of the wicked,
but I find "deadly weapons" difficult to accept!
In contrast, there are words
like those in Psalm 139, which are comforting and inspiring –
"Whither shall I go from thy spirit?
or whither shall I flee from thy presence?
If I ascend up into heaven, thou art there:

if I make my bed in hell, behold, thou art there.
If I take the wings of the morning, and
dwell in the uttermost parts of the sea;
Even there shall thy hand lead me,
and thy right hand shall hold me."
But, even in the same Psalm, we have
"Surely thou wilt slay the wicked, O God"!
There are those who tell us that we must regard every part
of the Bible as holy and verbally inspired by you,
as if you had dictated all these words
to those who wrote them down.
I am sorry, Lord, but,
while I do value the Bible immensely,
I cannot accept that.
Am I wrong to look at the Scriptures with such a critical eye?

No, of course you are not, My child.
Why do you think I gave humankind
intelligence and the power to reason?
The Bible is rightly called "God's Word",
but it must be realised that
it was not dictated to those who wrote.
Yes, I inspired them to write.
What I had to say was communicated
through their thinking and through
the circumstances they were facing;
it was, of course, related to such faith as they had in me.
Sometimes what they wrote was also influenced
by what the writer hoped might happen:
after all, they were human.
That is surely the case with some of the Psalms.
You must see in those parts which don't seem to inspire you,
the "humanness" of the writers.
Just like you, they were trying to make sense out of life,
as they related it to their faith in me.

Think also of some of the Old Testament prophets:
I challenged them to think seriously
about the events surrounding them -
events which were threatening the security of their people
so they were inspired to say to their contemporaries,
"thus saith the Lord".
Sometimes my words were mixed up with their desires –
sometimes desires for vengeance on those causing the threats.
Their words were not always
a true reflection of my will or my intention,
but they are still worth reading and
worthy of your reflection.
Many of them showed great insight
into the nature of my being and my will.
Don't ever take words or phrases out of their context:
that will only result in a very distorted image of
what I am really like:
never lose sight of the fact that,
even when there are words which are expressing anger,
always, love is my dominating characteristic.
"The Word" which is important above all the rest is
"The Word" portrayed in the opening chapter of John's Gospel!
My most important word is Jesus –
my living Word in whom I became a human being and,
"full of grace and truth", lived among you.
You saw his glory, - my glory -
Above all the printed word, He is "the Word"
whom you must treasure and respect and love.

Campbell Miller

Reading The Bible (2)

Lord, I was reading recently that,
the so-called "Jefferson Bible"
is being republished in America.
As you know, that third President of the USA
had problems with much that was in the Bible.
He regarded the ethical teaching of Jesus
recorded in the New Testament as the finest in the whole world,
but, he believed the Gospels had been manipulated
and in transmission, the true words and message of Jesus
became distorted by what he called
"the rubbish in which it is buried".
He also had very strong reservations
about much of the Old Testament.
So, with such objections about parts of the Bible,
he cut out all those verses which, in his opinion,
were unreasonable to believe and
which he considered were
exaggerated accounts of what really happened.
While I would never want to go as far as that,
I do have a certain sympathy with him!
But what a wealth of wonderful stories we would lose
if we followed his example!
I imagine that among those passages he cut out,
there would be the early chapters of Genesis.
I would hate to lose these wonderful Creation stories .
I certainly cannot take them literally –
I cannot believe that these are descriptions of
how life and the world began.
Science presents us with a different story of our origins:
I find that just as wonderful as the Genesis tale.

For me, the few opening words of the Genesis story
are the most significant –
"In the beginning, God…"
I would apply these same words
to any other account of how life began.
There is great mystery here and
even the most detailed and exhaustive scientific explanations
do not completely fathom the mystery –
I am glad that the mystery remains.
I feel sure that must be the way you want it to be
My faith can continue to hold to that simple statement –
"In the beginning, God…"
I am so grateful to those unknown characters who,
centuries ago, undoubtedly through your inspiration,
developed these superb stories:
they tried to find some explanation for their existence:
they sought to account for the wonderful world around them, and
they found the answer in you.
Lord, I know there are many who disagree with that view:
I once took the stories literally but,
I can no longer and I find it impossible to believe
that you would want me to!

My child, I would want you to be true
to what your own reason tells you.
But do not scorn those who disagree with you!
You do have common ground –
you both agree that, "in the beginning, God…"
You both agree that I am the Creator God.
There is room for various ideas of how I created!
·The important issue for you all is
how you respond to me as the Lord,
the Creator God who gives you life.

Lord, as I read again these early Genesis stories
I am so impressed with the insights of those who wrote them.
They did not have scientific knowledge
such as there is in today's world,
but they did understand a great deal about human nature:
that certainly hasn't changed over the centuries!
I think of how, in the story, Adam blames Eve
for his wrong doing and, indirectly blames you by saying,
"The woman *you* put here with me,
gave me the fruit, and I ate it."
I am afraid that still today,
we try to blame others for our mistakes, and, -
even blame you!
The writers, through the stories they wrote,
also made us aware of Divine justice –
Disobedience resulted in banishment from the garden!
They also wrote their story of a flood
to reflect their belief that you challenge
the sinfulness of humanity:
But also that you are compassionate –
they account for their continuing existence
by telling their story of Noah.
Lord, thank you for inspiring such stories:
for helping us, through them,
to gain insights into the wonder of your eternal being.

My child, they are wonderful stories
which have eternal truths within them.
They do show insights into human nature,
they do have within them aspects of my divine nature.
How sad it is that so many
who call themselves my people,
fall out with one another about how they regard such stories.
Some want to insist that the stories are "true"!
It is important to appreciate the difference

between stories which are "true"
and those which "convey a truth".
How I wish that instead of the bitter arguments,
you could all reflect more and more about
the truths which they convey –
truths about me, my nature,
my love for my creation.
Even in these early stories,
there is implicit my over-riding love.
Never lose sight of that.

Christian Unity

Lord, in that wonderful chapter 17 in John's Gospel,
we have the words of your prayer for your disciples:
presumably this is how these hopes lived on in their memory
and they have been preserved for us,
for which we are truly grateful.
The words
"that they may be one as we are one"
are often quoted when we think about Christian unity
in the context of all our various different churches –
Catholic, Anglican, Orthodox, Reformed, Baptist,
to mention only a few.
If I go to hospital as an in-patient, I am asked about my religion.
If I say "Christian" that probably will not be enough!
They want to know am I Roman Catholic, C of E, Baptist,
or some other denomination.
Should we all abandon our different emphases,
give up our various labels and simply be –
"Christians", all offering our worship in the same pattern?
(Of course, Lord, it would have to be in the way that is right for me!
The others would have to appreciate that they were wrong!!)
What were you praying for, Lord?
Of course all these divisions did not exist then!
How should we take these words now?
Are our different ways of worshipping and organising our churches
something which you condemn?
When we observe the Week of Prayer for Christian Unity,
Should our aim be to get rid of all our separate denominations?
Is that the kind of unity which you want?
Quite frankly, Lord, I really can't see that happening!

My child, neither can I!
That was not what I had in mind at all.
It is unity of spirit and purpose that I want, not uniformity.
Of course there are a variety of ways in which
worship can be offered:
of course there are different ways
in which fellowships can organise themselves:
of course there are numerous ways in which
the Gospel can be proclaimed.
The unity for which I prayed and for which I still pray
is the unity of love.
It would be good if people learned from each other
instead of judging.
There is such a variety of ways
in which I can be worshipped,
in which I can be served,
in which the message of my love can be shared.
Sometimes I feel I am regarded as
a Roman Catholic God, or
an Anglican God, or
a Baptist or Reformed God,
or in a variety of other ways!
But I am the Lord!
The Lord who longs for the worship of all,
however it is expressed!
I am the Lord who loves them all:
I am the Lord whose command to them all will always be,
"Love one another as I have loved you".

Anxiety and Grief

Lord, my beloved is seriously ill, in the hospital Critical Care Unit.
I am sitting with her,
confused by all the tubes and wires
linking her to the medical equipment.
Earlier today I was browsing through some prayers:
one prayer seemed to leap out from the page
for it was so appropriate to our situation.
"Lord, when we feel afraid and nothing seems secure or sure:
when we are tempted to give up or to turn elsewhere, cling fast to
us and hold us close until we feel again, the steady, unstoppable
beat of your love and the security of our place with you. Give us
the faith to trust profoundly that there is no suffering so deep that
your powerful love cannot transform it."
I scribbled it down and wondered -
could I read it to her without losing control of my emotions.
I did - and was so pleased when, later, she said to me,
"Will you read that prayer to me again?"
It obviously had meant a great deal to her.
I hope it somehow strengthened her faith and
made her more aware of that "unstoppable beat of your love".
Lord, I have to confess that having faith
in such a situation is far from easy:
My dominant emotion was one of deep anxiety.
I see myself rather like that man who,
when he brought his son to you for healing told you,
"I do have faith, but not enough: help me to have more".

My child, of course faith is not easy:
especially when you are torn apart by anxiety.
But your very act of praying, however hesitantly,

was your faltering faith showing itself.
Never forget that I too faced such crises of faith –
think of my prayers in Gethsemane!
Think again of what it was that you prayed:
of course you hoped for healing, but
you were realistic and,
sensibly, you asked instead
for reassurance of my presence and my love.
Although your faith is wavering,
be assured that both you and your loved one
are surrounded by my love.
However weak your faith, I am with you.
Nothing can ever change that.

Facing Death (1)

Lord, she was lying there in that small, hospital room:
I had been with her all day but she slept:
her breathing was laboured and
I felt that the end was near,
though I still told myself that I could be wrong.
I whispered to her, that same prayer which I had prayed with her
before in her seriously ill condition,
asking you to " cling fast to us and hold us close
until we feel again, the steady, unstoppable beat of your love
and the security of our place with you"..
Did she hear me, Lord?
You alone know!
It helped me, though, to be honest,
I am not sure how strongly
I really did feel "the beat of your love"!
Towards evening, Lord,
her breathing suddenly seemed to die away, and she was gone.
My emotions were so confused!
I looked lovingly at her and strangely,
I felt more aware than ever before
of the mystery which life really is.
I found myself asking,
"Where are you now, my love?
Are you gone for ever?"
None of the traditional views of "Heaven" came to mind:
In the ensuing days, all sorts of doubts troubled me
there were so many confusing reflections,
Lord, I feel that you understand.
Of course, I do wish you hadn't taken her,
but I do thank you for ending her suffering.

My faith is telling me, that she is with you –
whatever that means!
Lord, I do believe –help me, that my faith may grow stronger.

Yes, My child, she is with me –
and I am with you also, all the time.
You know you can trust me.
Remember also that this sorrow you are feeling
is all an inevitable part of loving and being loved.
Be mindful of that poem
you have often quoted to others – it applies to you also!
 "If love should count you worthy and should deign one day
 to be your guest, Pause ere you draw the bolt and bid him
 rest, if in your old content you would remain,
 for not alone he enters;
 in his train are angels of the mists,
 the lonely guest, dreams of the unfulfilled and unpossessed,
 and sorrow, and life's immemorial pain.
 He wakes desires you never may forget;
 he shows you stars you never saw before;
 he makes you share with him for evermore the burden of the
 world's divine regret.
 How wise you were to open not;
 and yet, how poor if you should turn him from the door."
You wisely chose to open the door:
some sadness now is a small price to pay
for the joy of loving and
the precious gift of being loved.

Facing Death (2)

Lord, today I had to break the news
to others that my beloved has passed away.
It was hard.
I know there was a tremor in my voice as I spoke.
Some of them had been very close to her:
they had known of her illness,
but I hesitated to upset them with sad news.
Lord, I needn't have worried.
I could feel the warmth of their loving concern
and the sharing of my grief –
it was real and though it brought more tears to my eyes,
it also gave me strength.
My missing her was not unique to me!
They, too, would miss her friendly smile -
her loving friendship.
Some of these friends have faith, some do not,
yet, somehow I was aware of your comforting strength and love
surrounding me through them all,
whatever they themselves believed.
I look back to my praying, that
you would "cling fast to us and hold us close"
I confess again that I had not really felt you near me,
in spite of telling myself that you were.
But you were close to me through these many friends:
I should have appreciated,
more than I sometimes do, that so often,
awareness of your mysterious, loving presence
comes through other people.
Someone expressed the view that in my grief
I would be finding comfort from "God's Word".

I have to confess that reading the Bible
was rather low on my priorities!
Was I wrong to feel like that?
No doubt in my quieter moments,
some well known verses from Scripture did come to mind,
but it was real, live, caring people
who gave me strength.
Does that in any way offend you Lord?

No, My child. I not only speak through the written word.
How much more real is my presence
when I show myself to you,
not in some ghostly, shadowy form,
but in another person, just like yourself –
how much more real is my voice,
when you hear it as they speak
their words of comfort to you?
Remember that powerful passage
in the first chapter of John's Gospel

> **" In the beginning was the Word, and the Word was with**
> **God, and the Word was God. The same was in the beginning**
> **with God. All things were made by him; and without him**
> **was not any thing made that was made….. And the Word was**
> **made flesh, and dwelt among us, (and we beheld his glory, the**
> **glory as of the only begotten of the Father) full of grace and**
> **truth."**

It was in real flesh and blood that I came to your world!
How else could I adequately
make folk aware of the reality of my love?
It is still through human voices
and human compassionate actions
that I speak to you – and will continue to do so.

Beyond This Life

Lord, the loss of my beloved has brought home to me that this is
perhaps the greatest mystery which we all have to face –
the mystery of death!
We know that it is ahead of us all -
we wonder what lies beyond.
We Christians talk about the "Christian Hope", -
mostly that is a somewhat vague expression:
for most of us it is enshrouded in mystery,
yet we cling to it, believing that
you must have something in store for us.
I find it impossible to believe that your love
which I have experienced through life,
will suddenly come to an end.
I find it impossible to believe that
the precious, loving relationships
which have been enjoyed in life,
come to an end with death, never to be shared ever again.
Lord, when friends offer comfort,
telling me that my beloved's parting from me is only for a time,
of course I want to believe it.
But as I try to imagine the nature of a life beyond,
the mystery of it all fills me with confusing doubts.
I remember some of the things you said -
words usually quoted as words of comfort at a funeral:
    "Let not your heart be troubled:
    you believe in God, believe also in me.
    In my Father's house are many mansions: if it were not so,
    I would have told you. I go to prepare a place for you.
    And if I go and prepare a place for you, I will come again,

and receive you unto myself; that where I am, there you may be also."
But the mystery remains.

My child, of course it is mystery!
Just as life itself is an adventure in which
the future is hidden from you,
so it must be with what lies beyond.
There are for you, hints in the Gospels
such as the verses you have quoted.
What you call "the Christian hope" is emphasised
for you again and again in the New Testament -
people like Paul and others
express their thoughts about this.
Think of the deep conviction expressed by Paul
when he wrote to the Roman Church,
> **"I am persuaded, that neither death, nor life, nor angels,**
> **nor principalities, nor powers, nor things present,**
> **nor things to come, nor height, nor depth, nor any**
> **other creature, shall be able to separate us from the**
> **love of God, which is in Christ Jesus our Lord."**
Think of the countless others in every generation who,
in one way or another have given expression
to their conviction that death is not the end –
Do you really think I would be playing a game with you all,
by letting you hope for that which does not exist?
Accept the mystery - continue to trust me.
Remember too, the words which Paul
quoted to the Corinthians from the Prophet Isaiah,
> **"Eye hath not see, nor ear heard, neither have entered**
> **into the heart of man, the things which God has**
> **prepared for them that love him."**

Take such words as coming from me –
the mystery, eventually, will be revealed.
The future is safe with me.

Campbell Miller

Coping With Sympathy

Lord, I have received so many letters and cards
expressing sympathy.
I treasure them all, though I am glad to be alone as I open them:
they bring a lump to my throat and tears to my eyes.
They tell me how much I am in the thoughts -
the prayers of so many friends and acquaintances;
they say such nice things about my loved one,
expressing so many wonderful memories.
I find myself talking to her:
"Why are you not here so that I can share these with you?
I am sure you didn't know how much these folks loved you -
now, neither they nor I can tell you
I often told you of my love for you -
did I really let you know how proud I was
to have you as my life's companion?"
Lord, am I being foolish when I think like that?

My child, you are reacting in the most natural way
to the loss you are feeling.
Indeed, these occasions
when your emotions are stirred so deeply,
are a reflection of the strong bond between you -
a tribute to the depth of your love for each other.
Be grateful for the warmth of real friendship
coming through such expressions of sympathy:
realise that I am speaking My words of comfort through them.
Can I suggest to you that through your grief
there is always a lesson to be learned? –
While your friends and loved ones are still with you,
let them know by your words and your actions,

how much they are valued by you.
Don't wait till they too have passed away!

Appreciating That Others, Too, Are Grieving

Lord, I am sorry, but I am feeling rather low today!
I suppose I shouldn't – after all,
I still have the support of friends and family:
above all, you have assured me of your presence:
In spite of that, loneliness seems to invade my life.
I go into town, do some shopping, which I don't really need:
being in the busyness of town, seems better than brooding at home.
I always find other people interesting!
Suddenly, as I look around,
I realise that so many of these folk
must also have their burdens to bear –
many of them must also be coping with sorrow!
I am not the only one who is feeling sad!
Then I notice some who are smiling and
I begin to feel myself smiling too!
How selfish of me to think that
my sadness is in any way unique!

My child, I understand
Your sadness is indeed not unique
but it is your sadness!
Of course such feelings come over you –
it would be very strange if they didn't.
I am glad you remember the power of a smile!
You too, can bring some cheer to many of the folks
who brush shoulders with you, by your smile.
You can't invade their privacy
by asking them why they are sad, or
by buttonholing them to tell them that I care about them!
That generally would be totally unproductive!

But a simple smile may help to lift their spirits.
Don't think of me as the One with a serious, pious expression –
I am also the God with a smiling, friendly face!

Music

Lord, I have just been listening to the final
of the Young Musician of the Year:
I found it deeply moving!
Such talent! Such wonderful music!
The experience somehow made me aware of your presence
for you must be behind the creation
of such joyous sounds and, indeed,
be behind such dedication to producing these glorious notes!
Music is such a mystery is it not?
Why should it be that a particular combination of notes
becomes so attractive and so moving,
while a different combination of the same notes
does not speak to me at all:
may even irritate me and appear as a jarring sound?
It is not surprising that for centuries,
music has played an important part in our lives.
It has given birth to inspiring thoughts and ideas,
uplifting our spirits, enriching our lives, -
stimulating many of us to worship you:
It has become the medium through which
we often express our worship.
It is not just glorious sounds
such as Handel's "Hallelujah Chorus" which I have in mind,
but simple tunes which echo in the memory and bring joy.
Lord, from the bottom of my heart, I thank you for the wonderful,
mysterious, enriching power of music.

**My child, I am glad that you find music
so stimulating and enriching -
also that you appreciate the mystery of it.**

Part of the mystery, of course,
is the fact that some of the sounds
which you find irritating or jarring,
are those which others enjoy!
Do not despise them!
The world of pop music is also responding
to my gift, enriching lives just as much as the classics!
I may not always approve of the sentiments
expressed in some of the songs,
but then, there are some of the hymns
which you sing which also
do not always meet with my approval!
But, music is music and
whatever the way in which it is expressed,
it clearly brings joy and enrichment to many lives
And I, the Lord of all, rejoice in that.

Other Faiths.

Lord, my community is one in which
many different faiths are represented:
there are Hindu Temples, Sikh Gurdwaras, Muslim Mosques,
Buddhist Temples, to mention only a few.
I enjoy living in such a community
with the richness of varying cultures -
different ways of expressing human spirituality.
I have been able to visit many of such places of worship -
I have enjoyed contact with numerous people of these faiths –
wonderful, caring people
whose devotion and sincerity is obvious –
in many cases more obvious than that
of some us who are Christians!
We have an annual service of "Prayers for Peace"
in which most of these faith groups play a very active part:
I find myself on such occasions,
being inspired and filled with hope:
I know the view of some of my fellow Christians -
They think our reason for association with these other faiths
should be to convert them to our Christian faith!
Should that really be my aim?
Is my faith the only right one?
Is the way in which I worship you the only true way?
Do you accept a Hindu prayer, like this,
just as much as any prayer I may offer?

> "From the unreal, lead me to the real,
> From darkness lead me to light,
> From death lead me to immortality.
> May God prosper both of us at the same time,

> At the same time support us both.
> May both of us at the same time apply our strength
> May there be no hatred between us
> May all here be happy
> May all be free from disease
> May nobody experience misery
> Peace, peace, peace."

Do you accept the devotions of the Muslims
who prostrate themselves before you five times each day
Does it matter that they call you by a different name?

**My son, do you really think
that I would turn a deaf ear to such prayers?
Do you really think that I would ignore
such devotion when it is sincerely offered?
There are different paths which lead to me.
Don't allow yourself to become judgemental:
No one has the monopoly of the truth –
It is so sad – so destructive of peace and harmony
when individuals or groups consider
that they alone are right.
By all means continue to have fellowship
with those whose beliefs differ from yours –
whose expressions of devotion and worship
are different to yours –
You may learn something from them!
You may catch some of their enthusiasm –
They may learn something from you!
Certainly, by your contact with them
you will be making a contribution
to peace and understanding.
Remember – when I told you to love your neighbour
that meant people of every faith and of none:
Love must not erect barriers –**

**Love must overcome those which exist.
Indeed, it is love
and love alone which can overcome them.**

Campbell Miller

Forgiveness

"Forgive us the wrongs we have done,
As we forgive the wrongs that others have done to us".
Lord, so easily we use these words in the prayer you taught us!
We are not very good at forgiveness!
I hear of tragic situations in which,
due to criminal activity, loved ones have been lost -
There is a cry for revenge,
masked somewhat superficially
by the words, "justice must be done".
I ask myself – if I was the victim –
or closely involved with the victim,
how would I feel?
I may be critical of those who thirst for revenge –
How would I react?
Would I be able to pray as you did from the cross –
"forgive them: they don't know what they are doing" ?
At a less dramatic level, but, no less real and disturbing,
I know of relationships soured and broken for ever,
because of a refusal to forgive.
Forgiveness is not an easy road to follow, -
there is pain in it.
It is not easy to deny ourselves
the satisfaction of retaliation:
there is the rather perverse pleasure of
responding with cold cutting words,
to say nothing of vengeful action.
The theory of forgiveness is fine, but when we are hurt,
we want to hit back –
we want our resentment to be felt.
I know it is such a complex issue!

If a serious crime has been committed,
justice should be done!
But, I am also filled with sadness
When I see some destroy their lives even further
by nursing bitterness and hatred
Lord, You forgave those who put you on the cross -
help me to appreciate, the healing power of forgiveness.
Teach me how to forgive.

My child, forgiveness is painful:
I know the pain of forgiveness –
Remember, not only the cross -
Remember, too the many times when I was rejected.
My offer of love still meets with rejection –
how often is my offer of loving forgiveness ignored -
How sad I am when I hear the prayer I taught,
recited without awareness of its significance;
"forgive us our sins as we forgive those who sin against us."
Can you really expect my forgiveness
while nursing a bitter grudge against another?
If a deep injury has been suffered,
there can be no real recovery
until there is forgiveness.
That does not mean ignoring the wrong –
it does mean overcoming the barrier to a relationship –
it does mean reaching out to a fresh start.

Lord, when I think about forgiveness,
I find myself thinking of the Coventry Cathedral –
The two words on the altar in the ruins of the old cathedral –
"Father forgive".
The wonderful symbolic design never fails to inspire!
The ruins - the result of devastating bombing raids –
By their side, the new cathedral,
rising as it were from the ashes of the old –

a constant reminder of the devastation of war:
"Father forgive"!
What did they mean by setting these words there?
Forgive those who caused the devastation?
Forgive those who sent the planes with the bombs?
Forgive the awful suffering and loss of life?
Surely we should realise that
the words issue a challenge to us all –
"Father, forgive us all for allowing such tragedies to happen –
Forgive us all for our failure which allows
anger, greed, hatred, selfishness, -
so many other negative emotions to dominate humankind –
encouraging war – banishing peace!"

**My child, it makes me sorrowful
if this is seen only as a generous and benevolent
expression of forgiveness to those
who at that time were the enemy.
I return to my tearful emotions expressed
on the slopes of the Mount of Olives
as I gazed at Jerusalem -
I utter my heartfelt cry to the contemporary world –
"would that even today you learned
those things which make for peace!"
Learning to forgive is an essential part of
those things which make for peace
It is a lesson you all need to learn.**

Campbell Miller

The Commandments

Lord, I have been reflecting on the Ten Commandments:
I suppose so many aspects of life today
suggest, to some that they are outdated and irrelevant.
Yet, there can be no denying that
if only the principles embedded in them were accepted –
if only we all lived by these principles,
the world would certainly be a happier place.
Thank you Lord, for giving us these rules
through Moses, all these centuries ago.
I know that the Old Testament
portrays in a dramatic way how these were given
at the sacred mount of Sinai –
"written by the finger of God on tablets of stone"!
I prefer to think of it happening in the less dramatic,
but more acceptable way as you inspired Moses
in his thinking and planning for his people–
I wonder who it was who carved the words on the stones!
Could it have been Moses himself?
Of course I know that such speculation is irrelevant!
I have no doubt whatsoever that the rules came from you.
How wonderful it is that these rules –
these moral and spiritual principles have
continued to be the basis of civilised human society.
I am so glad we have them –
I am only too aware that I have not observed them all –
forgive me, Lord.
I am even more glad when I read your words in the Gospel
"A new commandment I give to you,
that you love one another, as I have loved you"
Mind you – that is even more challenging -

It certainly sums up all the rest.
But, can we really love to a command?

**My child, no, neither I nor
anyone else can force you to love!
It is an aim to set before you:
love one another –
love your neighbour as yourself.
I am not talking about emotional love –
That, especially cannot respond to a command:
It is caring – love in action:
That is the response for which I look.
The old rules still stand as important reminders, -
important principles for life – but,
the New Commandment is more important:
keep that aim constantly before you –
Love one another –
There can be no other way but Love.**

Advent and Christmas

Lord, It's that time of year again!
The shops, as usual, much too early with all their Christmas fare!
I start to think about the presents which will have to be bought!
What did I buy them last year?
Cards to be written –
did I receive one from them last year?
It's not always easy to maintain the true Christmas spirit!
So much pressure on those who cannot really afford it -
to spend, spend, spend
"It's alright: it's on my credit card"!
Sadly, they may still be paying it off, next Christmas!
We eat too much – and drink too much,
telling ourselves, "well – it is Christmas!"
Perhaps I am beginning to sound like Scrooge!
"Humbug!"
In spite of what I say, I do enjoy Christmas –
The carols, the Christmas Tree, the lights in town, but -
what has all this to do with you being born at Bethlehem?
It is now so commercialised.
I remember as a student working on the Christmas post
hearing a young woman say,
"How I hate these religious Christmas cards!
Now, in fact it is not always easy
to buy cards which refer to your birth at all!
Lord, it's your festival – your birthday, -
You seem to have been pushed out from it.
Not only was there no room for you at the inn,
There appears to be little room for you
in our Christmas!
We sing the carols,

smile at the children's nativity plays – but,
lose sight of what is at the heart of it all –
you coming to share our humanity -
coming to demonstrate the power of your love for us.
We forget that Christmas is about the birth of one
who was born to die!
Born in the humblest surroundings –
a squalid stable, the place of the animals –
born to die in the humiliation and suffering of the cross -
such contrast with our parties,
our crackers, our lavish meals!
Lord, forgive us!

My child, I don't want you to be miserable!
By all means celebrate Christmas.
For many it is a bright, cheerful spot
in the midst of the darker days of winter.
But, of course, you are right:
so much of the celebration disappoints me.
yet, each year there are signs of hope!
Unselfish acts of kindness,
sacrifices made for those facing real hardship:
some looking beyond the glitter and tinsel,
less earth-bound than others,
seeking, even if in a half-hearted way,
some more lasting meaning in it all:
trying, though they would not describe it in these terms,
to understand "the Incarnation"!
For that is what is at the heart of the true Christmas –
Immanuel! God with you!
The mystery of the Incarnation!
My, coming to share the real experience of humanity -
That is the Christmas message -
you must go on sharing with the world:

the message of my love –
the message of hope.

Campbell Miller

Lent

"Lord, observing Lent is not very easy!
Giving up something important to me is really quite hard –
I might manage it for a few days –
well, maybe one day!
But forty days?
What should I have given up?
Cake, chocolates, using the car!
That would be difficult!
Stop being critical of other people?
I know I should be doing that anyway!
Then there's this suggestion that instead of giving up –
or - as well as giving up,
I should be "taking up";
taking up something extra:
perhaps, making a special effort to be of service to others:
giving to charity which cares -
or being more loyal to my church…
Lord, what do you think?
Is it really necessary to observe Lent in some way?

No, My child, - not necessary.
But certainly good for your soul –
maybe good for your body as well!
I can make many suggestions,
most of which you already know
but, have put to the back of your mind –
Of course it is not easy:
nothing which is truly worthwhile is easy!
Remember that the forty days of Lent

are to remind you of the time I spent alone
in the lonely wilderness near to Jericho.

Lord, when you say that,
I remember standing on the outskirts of Jericho,
by a wonderful wayside fruit stall
with such a colourful display of fresh fruit
which made my mouth water,
but, as I glanced away to my left,
I saw the bare, desolate area
which I am told is where you spent these forty days. –
such a forbidding place -
no fruit to refresh you –
nothing to alleviate your hunger and thirst!
I should have been reflecting on your situation,
instead of admiring the lovely fresh fruit I could buy!
Now, instead of moaning about the hardship
of trying to observe Lent
I should be wondering what other sacrifices I could make!

Yes, they were tough days,
described, as you know, as "my Temptations".
I had to think my way through
to how I must achieve what is required of me.
My temptation was to find an easy way
of demonstrating the power of love –
an easy way of attracting people to follow me –
but there is no easy way -
I had to commit myself to the way of the Cross:
the ultimate way of expressing love.
This is how far I go to convince you of the reality of that love.
Do you think that these forty days were easy for me?

Lord, you make me feel ashamed -
my efforts are pathetic when compared to what you endured.

You told your followers that they should be prepared
to take up their cross and follow you.
You were never one for "giving up!"
I can see that "taking up" is much more positive:
what is the cross that you expect me to take up?

My child, you know very well what it is!
You know very well that it may vary from day to day
as you become aware of the varying demands
that life makes on you.
Of course it is not easy, -
it was never intended that life should be easy –
how dull it would be if it was!
Do you remember Simon, who was forced by the soldiers,
to carry my cross on that awful journey to Calvary?
In a sense, I am like him –
sharing the burden of your cross,
but, where he had that burden forced upon him,
I share yours willingly and lovingly:
I am always by your side.

Campbell Miller

Weeping Over Jerusalem

Lord, as you approached Jerusalem,
you must have been tempted to turn back –
head up once again to the peace of Galilee
where you had many, great successes.
Your disciples tried to persuade you not to go to the city.
you attempted to make them aware of the troubles which lay ahead -
Peter made you angry:
his words came to you as a powerful temptation –
you even called him "Satan"!
Then you stood on the slopes of the Mount of Olives
looking across at the city.
I have stood in the little chapel which commemorates this –
they call it "The Chapel of Dominus Flevit",
the place where the Master wept -
the place where you stood gazing over at the city,
weeping, as you felt such sorrow
that the things which make for peace had not been learned.
In my mind, I still can feel myself standing there today-
aware of the tension and the strife in that wonderful land –
the place where you displayed your love –
aware too of the hatred and strife
in so many places around the world.
I find myself reflecting on the deep sorrow
which you still must feel –
a sorrow which never fades –
a sorrow which is part of the price of love.
Lord, I try to share your sorrow – but I know,
the depth of my sorrow fades
into insignificance in comparison to yours.

Campbell Miller

Yes, My child, my sorrow is still real –
as I look out on, not just the city of Jerusalem,
but the whole world of today,
it is still my heartfelt wish that you would all learn
the ways of peace instead of strife –
the way of love instead of hatred.
You may even shed an occasional tear
for the tragic situations of blind prejudice which divides, -
the greed which brings starvation and death, -
the bitter anger which seeks revenge, -
but tears need to turn into love –
love needs to be translated into action.
We still have such a long way to go until that becomes reality!
I so much need your help,
the help of all my people, not just to be moved to tears
but to walk more closely the path of love -
to face up to the demands of love.

Palm Sunday

I wonder, Lord,
as you moved down the slopes of the Mount of Olives,
what was in your mind?
I reckon your disciples certainly must have become excited -
optimistic in spite of trying
to persuade you not to come to Jerusalem.
There you were, now sitting on the back of a donkey,
riding into the city amid shouts of welcome!
Your friends must have thought –
"This is more like the way it should be!
You were clearly mistaken with all
that talk of trouble – even of death!"
The crowds are shouting "Hosanna!" –
they can't do enough to show
that they think you are the Messiah –
you are welcome!
If I try to close my mind to what I know
followed in the next few days,
I too, can let myself be caught up in this enthusiasm –
it is all going to alright!
What can possibly go wrong after a welcome like this!
Then, you go and spoil it all!
You go to the temple and, blazing with anger,
you chase away the men who are exploiting
the worshippers by charging outrageous prices
for sacrificial animals.
You challenge those who are forcing worshippers
to change their Roman money for special temple coins –
to pay their temple dues,
again at an outrageously high price.

If the Gospel narrative is right, you even became violent!
How dismayed and angry your friends must have been -
worried too – anxious for you – and for themselves,
thinking that the authorities could not let you get away with it -
and they were known to be your close friends!
Even today, there are those who point to this incident,
suggesting that you were not really
the man of peace you professed to be.

Certainly I took what could be termed "violent action"!
I overturned the table of the money changers,
I waved the scourge of cords at the sacrificial animals -
I chased them away,
but I hurt no one physically –
I did hurt their pride - I hurt their profits:
I had to demonstrate my anger –
they were taking advantage
of people's sincere desire to worship.
My mind went back to what I saw
on that other day at the Temple
when I noticed many rich people
making a show of giving a lot of money.
Then a poor widow came up -
put in two coins worth only a few pennies.
She had put in more than all the others -
Everyone else gave what they didn't need:
she was very poor and gave everything she had.
How could I allow such people to be cheated and exploited?
No wonder I was angry!
In any case, you must not think that it was this action
which led to my arrest.
That was going to happen anyway.
Through the terrible events of the next few days,
love was being demonstrated –
love so great that it could not be expressed in any other way.

Lord, forgive me for thinking, like the disciples,
that you were spoiling the triumph!
Indeed, I wish I could show such courage
in the face of injustice.
There is certainly so much more
of the great mystery of divine love
which I still need to try to understand.
Help me Lord,
that my mind may always be open to you.

Campbell Miller

The Palm Cross

Lord, as I look ahead to the days of this Holy Week
there is fresh in my mind, our Palm Sunday worship.
I have my palm cross
in fact I have several of them from previous years.
I look at one of them -
it reminds me of that joyous procession in Jerusalem,
the palm branches being waved in welcome:
the words of one of our hymns comes to mind
    "Ride on, ride on in majesty,
    hark all the tribes "hosanna" cry.
    O saviour meek, pursue your way
    with palms and scattered garments strowed"
Then I remember that the next verse
focuses my thoughts on the other aspect of the palm cross –
    "Ride on, ride on in majesty
    in lowly pomp, ride on to die."
So then, I realise my simple Palm cross is pointing me
to the drama of the week ahead -
My palm cross is challenging me
to reflect on the sad, sad day of Friday -
the darkest day of them all,
when you are nailed to a cross of wood and left to die.
The image of that brings tears to my eyes:
thoughts of your words from that cross flash into my mind –
how you felt completely abandoned.
So, my palm cross, received so casually on Sunday
becomes an object of tragedy,
a conveyer of sadness,
a stimulator of such a variety of emotions.

Yes, My child, I am glad that the simple little cross
speaks to your faith like that:
there is something else that you have not mentioned –
your palm cross is empty –
there is no image of me hanging there.
You must also regard it as a symbol of hope:
a symbol of joy in the face of tragedy and sadness.
Good Friday is followed by Easter Day –
death could not destroy me –
my presence is always with you.
By all means, keep your Palm Cross –
let it remind you of all the drama of Holy Week –
let it continue to speak to you of me and my love –
let it continue to challenge you –
let it continue to remind you of my abiding presence with you –
I really am with you always.

Lord, thank you for that promise of your presence with me
I know I so often forget,
except in moments like this:
I am so ashamed that sometimes I ignore you!
Then, - as I look ahead to so many other dramatic events
which you still had to face
before the wonderful climax of Easter Day,
I am lost in wonder at the extent of your love -
my sense of shame grows.
Forgive me, Lord.

The Last Supper

Lord, I have been thinking about that last occasion
when you shared the Passover meal with your friends.
There appeared to be some secrecy
about making the arrangements:
perhaps because you were aware of
the tense atmosphere which was building up.
I am sure you had so many memories of all the times
in the past when you observed Passover with your family:
truly happy occasions
as you celebrated together the freedom gained
by your forefathers from slavery in Egypt.
I am sure also in all the other homes in the city,
as families observed Passover,
there was a strong element of hope that once again,
freedom would come – freedom from the rule of Rome.
I expect as you followed the usual ritual of Passover
there were the words,
"why is this night different from all other nights?" –
well, you certainly made this one very different indeed!
Your friends must have been somewhat confused by what followed!
As you took the bread and broke it
to pass it round the company, you told them,
"this is my body, given for you" –
they hadn't heard that before!
They were even more confused
when the cup was passed around and you said
"This is my blood of the new covenant which is shed for many."
Little did they realise
that these words would become a regular part of worship by
countless numbers of your followers for centuries to come!

You also told them that one of them would betray you!
Well, that certainly made it a very different night!

Yes, it was different,
but the time had come for the dream of freedom
to move on from political liberty.
These friends of mine had to begin to learn
that now, I would be their Passover!
They had to face the fact that
I was the Passover Lamb about to be offered -
the dominating aspect of it all was love -
the power of Divine love for them and for all humanity.

Lord, that focuses my attention
on the words often used when we celebrate communion –
"Christ our Passover is sacrificed for us".
Forgive me for the times when I share in the bread and wine,
casually or thoughtlessly:
too often, it has seemed like a routine part of my worship.
For me, also, when we gather at your table,
the occasion again should be so different –
I should be challenged by what we are doing:
"why is this occasion different from others?"
I should be more aware of the atmosphere of the Upper Room -
aware of all that you were trying to communicate
to your friends then –
what you want to communicate to me now
through bread and wine.

Yes, My child, let me again and again,
speak to your heart lovingly, through these simple
but profound symbols.
Come to the sacred table

with what measure of love you have:
You are truly welcome

Campbell Miller

Washing the Disciples' Feet

Lord, I feel I must talk to you about
your other strange action when you and your disciples
met in that Upper Room to celebrate Passover -
you insisted on washing the feet of your friends!
But that was a task for a servant:
The host would greet his guests,
but the servant would carry out the menial task –
removing the sandals, gently bathing the feet,
washing away the dust from the road.
Surely, this was not right!
You, the Master, kneeling down,
carrying out this lowliest of tasks.
No wonder Peter protested!
I am sure he, or one of the others
would have done this for you.
(though perhaps they might have argued
if you had asked them to do it for each other!)

My child, I am sure they would –
they still had so much to learn!
I wanted to do this for them!
I wanted, in a practical way
to emphasise what I had said to them
on several previous occasions:
"if one of you wants to be great,
he must be the servant of the rest"
They were good men –
I was proud to have them as my friends
but they were human!
They had so much to learn about the way of love –

as you all do!
You too, still "stand on your dignity"!
You want to serve me, but feel that
some tasks are beneath you –
You all need to take to heart the example I set
by being the servant – that is the way of love.
When you come to my table –
when you accept bread and wine –
remember that through these
down to earth, simple elements
I am challenging you to follow the way of a servant –
The way of love.
A new commandment I have given to you -
"that you love one another, as I have loved you".
I am the Servant Lord, who calls you again and again
To the only truly satisfying way of life –
Following the path of service –
the path of love.

Gethsemane

Lord, you went with your friends to the garden:
such a lovely, quiet peaceful place,
surrounded by olive trees –
olive branches which became a symbol of peace and reconciliation -
a good place to pray.
But that day, although the surroundings were peaceful,
there was such turmoil in your spirit –
such grief and anguish which came over you -
you knew the trouble which lay ahead.
You moved away from your friends and,
throwing yourself face downward on the ground, you prayed,
"My Father, if it is possible,
take this cup of suffering from me!"
How awful to be aware of the inevitability of what was to come!
I can only imagine
the depth of despair and the loneliness of rejection.
Do I detect a note of impatience –
disappointment in your voice,
when you return to your friends and find them asleep?
"How is it that you three were not able
to keep watch with me for even one hour?
Keep watch and pray that you will not fall into temptation."
But then you seem to understand and recognise that for them,
"the spirit is willing, but the flesh is weak"!
I feel sure that, as these men looked back on this
they must have had a deep feeling of sorrow and regret:
"We couldn't even stay awake
while He was in such agony of spirit:
how selfish and unfeeling we were!"
We who read about this are apt to criticise them -

yet I know in my heart -
I would probably have been no different!
Lord, if only we who are your followers today
could find your kind of courage and commitment!
Even in your despair, you can still pray,
"Not what I want, but what you want"!
We often seem to emphasise the awfulness
of your suffering on the cross –
of course it was real and so terrifying
but, perhaps we should be even more aware
of the mental and spiritual suffering which you experienced.
Some have said it was easy for you
because of your divine nature,
but you convince me that this was no sham:
you were experiencing just the same anguish
which any human would feel,
nevertheless, you could bow to the Divine will,
for only in that way could love triumph.
I know that there are times
when I too need to learn acceptance
but it is not easy!
Lord, teach me how to accept what you want in my life.

My child, it certainly was no sham.
I was definitely experiencing the depths of human anguish.
I could have rebelled against the divine will:
there was no pretending about my prayer
for this cup of suffering to be removed!
Believe me, it was a most heartfelt cry
from the despair I was feeling.
But love won the day!
I knew that the path ahead which I had to follow
was the only way to express
the depth and breadth of the divine love for humankind.

The Trial

Lord, I read again what the Gospels tell us
about that awful day when you were arrested
and dragged before Pontius Pilate, the Roman Governor.
For many, of course, it was an honour to be in his presence –
after all, he was appointed by the Emperor himself!
But this was different.
You were standing there is chains –
as if you would try to run away!
Was this really Roman justice?
I have been reading a novel about the life of Pilate -
when I think of him standing on judgement over you,
I must confess I feel a little sorry for him.
Certainly he was in a very difficult position:
your enemies were so determined for your death:
he did try to have you released.
He probably realized that the whole business was
a tragic miscarriage of justice -
possibly it haunted him for the rest of his life.
I try to imagine what it must have been like for you -
you whose whole life was one of love
Most facing such a situation would speak out -
would protest their innocence:-
would try to put the blame on their accusers –
but not you Lord!
No self-justifications – no attempt to persuade the Governor
that you had done nothing wrong –
You hardly said a word!
As I reflect on the scene, my emotions are all mixed up:
I feel anger with Pilate,
fury with your accusers,

deep fear and foreboding,
knowing how it will end: and yet also,
through my tears,
such admiration of your courage, and your faith.
And it all puts me to shame.

My child, remember, I faced none of this to win your admiration.
Of course it was all terrifying:
I knew what the outcome would be.
I witnessed the expressions of hatred
on the faces of my accusers -
aware of the ease with which they had stirred up the people-
Those same people who earlier,
had welcomed me with their shouts of "hosanna".
I was shocked by how easily they were persuaded
to choose the release of Barabbas –
a man who had a well-known criminal record.
All that hurt me just as much as the rough treatment I received
For I was truly sharing all that it means to be human –
physical pain, - but also
the devastating emotional pain of rejection and hatred,-
the shouts of "crucify him" seemed to be all around me.
But it had to be, if my love was truly to be expressed.

The Crucifixion

Lord, I reflect on that most tragic of scenes
at the place called Golgotha.
The deed has been done –
they have stretched you out over that cross -
hammered the nails through your hands and feet:
I can almost hear the thud of the hammer echoing in my mind –
it still makes me wince as I think of it.
I find myself still blazing with anger
at the mocking insults you had to bear.
Down there, at the foot of the cross, sit the soldiers,
they are throwing dice,
I see the one who threw the highest,
taking the robe which you wore:
these are the men who nailed you there, -
it has all made so little impression on them
that they can sit and gamble for your coat,
unmoved by the suffering they have caused,
oblivious to the agony being endured just above their heads:
still intent on personal gain.
And what is so disturbing is that
they were ordinary men just like us.
I don't doubt that the man who was lucky enough
to win the coat, went home later, proud of his prize,
showing it to his wife and family –
to those who loved him and regarded him
as a good husband and father.
Lord, as I gaze in amazement and with horror at this scene –
I ask myself - how different am I from them?
Then Lord, there are those others:
They are very different from the rough soldiers who mocked you:

they are the truly religious elite!
Pharisees, priests – the cream of the Jerusalem society!
How can they stoop so low?
But they are the ones who engineered this whole tragedy.
They are the ones who spurred on the crowds,
earlier in the day, to shout for your death.
They too find it all so amusing!
They hurl such insults at you
as they pace backwards and forwards by the cross,
looking up at you as they walk.
I hear their mocking words,
    "You who were going to pull down the temple
       and rebuild it within three days!
       If you are the anointed of God, as you say you are,
       come on down so that we may see it and believe" –
I hear their scornful laughter as they say it.
How Lord, can people faced with such awful suffering
be so heartless and unfeeling?
Then I ask myself,
"What if you had come down?
Would that really have been your victory?
Or would it have declared
that there are limits to your love?"

My child, there are no limits to the divine love:
Had the cross ended differently
that would have been the most terrible defeat of all –
love would have been defeated.
Think of these great words which
St Paul wrote to the Church at Rome
and have been such an inspiration
to countless followers over the centuries:
    " I am persuaded, that neither death, nor life,
      nor angels, nor principalities,
      nor powers, nor things present, nor things to come,

nor height, nor depth, nor any other creature,
shall be able to separate us from the love of God,
which is in Christ Jesus our Lord."
It was most surely the triumph of love
which was seen at Golgotha,
that terrible yet wonderful day!

Lord, I wonder about your friends
as they saw you breathe your last?
As they heard your cry from the cross –
"It is finished!"
Was it a quiet word of relief
which hardly anyone could hear – "my suffering is over"?
Was it like the final word from One
to whom life had become such a burden?
Surely not,
for your life, though so short could never have been a burden:
you lived it joyously for others.
You had your disappointments,
you had your moments of despair, as we all do,
but rejoicing that life was over?
Surely not!
It was no quiet, breathless, heaving sigh of relief –
it was a shout of triumph –
It is accomplished!
I have achieved what had to be done!
Even though your friends, so full of sadness,
thought that now all their dreams and hopes
would become just memories,
you knew that what you had achieved was so wonderful -
they too would soon discover that the best was yet to come –
soon they would realise that this was not the end,
but a glorious new beginning.

Joseph of Arimathea

Lord, I am thinking about Joseph of Arimathea,
who dares to approach Pilate,
asking for permission to bury your body.
A brave action!
Who would want to give a decent burial
to one who appears to have been condemned as a criminal?
I see him as an imposing figure: wealthy, influential!
A member of the Sanhedrin,
the same council which earlier had said that you must die.
Apparently he was already one of your disciples,
but secretly, for he was afraid of his influential colleagues.
Did he speak in your defence
when you were brought before the Council?
If so, there is no record of it!
But, clearly, what he had witnessed on this day
made all the difference to him:
throwing aside his fears, he comes into the open,
caring no longer what the other Council members think of him.
"Can I have the body, so that we can bury it?"
Surprisingly, Pilate gives permission and you are taken
to a tomb which was really the place where
Joseph himself had expected to be buried.
How courageous! No longer a secret admirer.
Perhaps overcome with sadness, not just with your death, -
sadness that he had given you no loyalty in life:
If he had spoken up before, would it all have been different?
How little did he know that his gift of a tomb –
a last resting place for One he so admired,
would become the eternal symbol of human hope –
for the tomb would be empty.

The sadness and gloom of today
would be transformed by the glory and triumph of Sunday: -
you are not dead, but alive for evermore!

My child, yes, I am grateful to Joseph,
not so much for his gift of a tomb –
did I really need a tomb?
Yes, I did – not for a permanent resting place
but for an eternal symbol of the power of love!
No, Joseph remained quiet in the Sanhedrin:
keeping his admiration for me from his colleagues:-
even from my other disciples!
Don't be hard on him –
he could be a secret disciple no longer:
regardless of the consequences
he declared himself for me.
Would you have had the courage to speak out in my defence?
Today - you must face the challenge –
are you known to be for me?

Resurrection

Lord, I have been reading a novel entitled
"the Skeleton in God's Closet".
The story is about an archaeologist who claims
to have discovered your body
and his claim is authenticated so well that,
when news of it breaks,
shock waves are sent around the whole of Christendom.
I find myself wondering how I would feel
if I woke up to headlines which stated -
"Easter has been cancelled!
The Body of Jesus has been found!"
How far would it matter to me if it was to be proved
beyond all doubt that the resurrection never happened?
Lord, you know the resurrection poses problems for many people:
I believe it with my heart,
but sometimes my head suggests something different!
Death is real!
It is clearly an inevitable part of being human -
if, as I believe, you truly and totally accepted
the restrictions and limitations of humanity,
how can it be that you come back to life again?
Some years ago in Scotland, I listened with a Junior School class
to a schools religious broadcast -
It was just before Easter.
In the course of it the presenter said,
"You too can prove for yourself that Jesus is alive!"
I was considerably disturbed at this being said
especially to children,
for there is no proof, is there Lord?

No, My child, as you know,
there are many aspects of life where proof is not possible.
No doubt the presenter spoke from the best of motives,
but it was unwise.
In such important matters like this,
you are in the realm of faith.
You can explore evidence - but evidence is not proof!
Do you think hardheaded sceptics like
Thomas and Saul of Tarsus were deluded?
They must have seen something enormously convincing.
Do you think it was easy for these first disciples
to accept the reality of the resurrection?
After all they had been present at the crucifixion –
they had the evidence of their own eyes!
The Gospel writers reflect clearly that it wasn't easy for them!
They too had problems with it.
They tell of many mixed reactions.
Matthew tells that some doubted,
Mark says that when the news was given
there was a mixture of fear and disbelief,
Luke describes the startled and terrified reaction
when I appeared among them,
John tells the classic story of Thomas the Doubter.
For all of them, regardless of what they had seen,
there was a leap of faith which had to be made
if they were to accept what had happened.
My child, take heart from this.
You cannot achieve cast iron certainties about matters of faith, -
faith is not like that –
but you know you can trust me!
Death has been conquered –
The victory is mine!

The Ascension

Lord, like so many, I am puzzled about
what we call your "ascension":
On Ascension Day, we think about you being
"taken up" back to Heaven.
Would it not have been better if you had remained?
We would not have had any doubts
about your resurrection then, would we?
Could you not have continued to make appearances
to your friends – and indeed,
to countless others who also could become your friends
by getting to know you in the flesh?
In our age of amazing technology, space travel
and fantasy tales such as those portrayed
in the adventures of Dr Who,
we are tempted to regard the Ascension
in a similar, rather sceptical way.
It presents a strange image
which leaves us feeling somewhat uncomfortable.
And yet, there must be some truth here
which challenges my faith.

My child, think more carefully about all this!
Do you really think that it would have been wise?
An ageless Christ, century after century,
flitting here and there around the world?
You remember that the Gospel tells you that
when I "ascended" –
left my disciples, there on the Mount of Olives,
they returned to Jerusalem with great joy -
continually they were in the Temple, blessing Me!

Surely, you would have expected them
to have turned homeward with leaden steps,
too sad for words to be spoken.
You would think that they would be
like folks irreparably bereaved.
You would not have been surprised if they returned to Galilee
resuming their old life style.
But this! Great joy!
That must surely make you wonder
what lies behind such a surprising reaction.
I had convinced them that now,
I would always be with them in Spirit.
Yes, they often forgot that - as you do!
But my resurrection and my ascension are bound together –
all part of the triumph of love:
this is how you, by faith,
really can know my presence with you today.
My ascension must not be regarded
as a kind of journey through space:
it was the change from what is seen to what is unseen –
from the world of time and space,
with which you are familiar,
to the less familiar, but very real world
which is all around but is not tied to time or space –
the world which responds to faith.

Pentecost

Lord, it is Pentecost,
that part of the Christian Year which
we find rather difficult to understand,
yet feel that it must be of some great significance.
We read about the "Day of Pentecost" in the Acts of the Apostles, -
much of this seems so remote from our experience -
a rather incomprehensible mystery
which, nevertheless, we feel bound to celebrate
in some way once a year?
We are told that they were gathered together –
folks who were living on the memories of three years
in which they had experienced
your physical presence and companionship.
The story is about a sudden strong wind, -
men apparently with a flame resting on each one, -
an upsurge of exuberance -
onlookers thought that they were drunk!
It was mysterious, not only to those who observed it
but also to those involved.
It is certainly enshrouded in mystery for us.
What are we to make of all that in our time?

My child,
remember what happened before this:
what you call "the Ascension".
There was the realisation that now their beloved master,
was set free, no longer bound to a particular place or time –
now His spirit would be with them all the time.
They were constantly at prayer together;
they were so concerned to keep alive what I meant to them.

You should be looking at the significance of all that;
this was not a divine imposition on unwilling participants.
I do not work that way!
I work by persuasion and my voice is the pleading of love.
You must not think of this as the birth of the Holy Spirit,
as if some new aspect of me had suddenly emerged.
Remember the Creation story in Genesis –
It was my spirit "moving over the face of the waters"
which was involved in Creation.
My Spirit has been the inspiration of
generations of people who responded to my prompting
since the beginning of time.
In the same way, on that day of Pentecost,
these who were committed to me were inspired, -
were ready to accept my empowering, -
they could now emerge with this new impetus
to be my people, my witnesses
to the transforming power of love.
This was my response to their commitment -
if there had been no such commitment and devotion
then Pentecost would not have happened!
This is the challenge of Pentecost to you today –
To be more truly, mine –
To be more truly my Church –
my witness for today.
I am depending on you.